ABOUT THE AUTHOR

Ankita Saxena is a British-Indian writer and performer. Her debut poetry collection Mother | Line is the culmination of over a decade of writing, editing and performing. She read English Literature at the University of Oxford (2014-2017), where she was Head of Events at Oxford University Poetry Society and President of Turl Street Arts Festival. She is a Barbican Young Poet alumnus, three-time commended Foyle Young Poet, part of the Octavia Poetry Collective, and one half of the ORIGINS Poetry Duo. Her poetry is published in Wasafiri, Modern Poetry in Translation, Bath Magg, Lacuna Lit and The Isis. She has performed widely across the UK, including live at Hammersmith Appollo, with The Guilty Feminist. By day, she works at a not-for-profit social enterprise, helping to tackle complex and enduring issues in society and create lasting and widespread change.

"A powerhouse of an anthology. Electric verse with a howling feminist soul. Bright. Witty. Poignant. Glorious. Ankita Saxena is an insightful, young artist and a voice that we need."

- Deborah Frances-White

"These poignant, muscular poems shoulder the weight of personal and national history. Uncompromising interrogations of empire and privilege sit alongside vivid evocations of family lore. Always remembering that 'our school / is our Ma's tongue', Saxena recognises women's stories, rituals and laughter for the precious gifts that they are."

- Natalie Linh Bolderston

"While Mother | Line touches on the traumas and complex inheritances of race, class, and gender, it's also able to hold onto child-like hope, particularly in its reflections on friendship. This book plants a seed of faith that, despite our tumultuous histories, we are able to grow into something better, as long as we keep looking for the things that truly need to be seen."

- Amani Saeed

"A sublime and considered collection, speaking to, and spanning lineage, inheritance, friendship; what it can mean to be a girl, a woman in the world -- across continents, oceans, time."

- Rachel Long

Ankita Saxena
Mother | Line

BIRMINGHAM

PUBLISHED BY VERVE POETRY PRESS
https://vervepoetrypress.com
mail@vervepoetrypress.com

FIRST PUBLISHED APR 2023

Printed and bound in the UK
by ImprintDigital, Exeter

ISBN: 978-1-913917-34-0

"Build of my poems
a bonfire in your backyard"
Kamala Das

CONTENTS

FOREWORD

Our names give us away.

For the most part, they explain who our fathers are. And their fathers. And their fathers' fathers.

In the steady passing down of names through generations, our mothers, and their mothers, and their mothers' mothers are gradually erased. Women are gradually erased.

*

These poems form a collective ode to the mother line. This line is cloudy, complex and often contradictory. The women who came before me passed on their fear *and* their fearlessness, their loving *and* their rage, their hunger *and* their shame.

Our mothers, and our mother lines are sacred – even as we forge new routes, friendships, relationships, mothers linger on the sides, hearing us become them: our routines only theirs to thank for, our spices, our blends and even our greedy tongues.

Even as it is obscured and often forgotten, the mother line is all-encompassing, inescapable.

*

My forever inspiration Zeina Hashem Beck writes:

> "Though we weren't a revolution,
> we were at least a questioning"

The same could be said for the collective "we" of the poems in *Mother | Line*. The poems here do not promise revolution, but they are at least an interrogation, a linguistic archaeology.

I have always been a questioner. The first poem I remember writing was on outer space – my first line in purple felt-tip, read something like:

"I wonder why the sky is so blue?"

I have long left behind questions on space for astrophysicists. But I have kept coming back to questions on identity and the micro-histories that combine to create us. Questions like the ones I ask Nani, who has tirelessly served another her whole marital life –

"Where are you looking in that red sari, gone brown?"
"Why don't you bring a girl close to your chest and call her daughter?"
"O won't you tell me you loved? Tell me you loved equally."

Through asking questions, we pose challenges. Through asking questions, we gradually chip away at stigma. All revolutions begin, and are cradled within, a question. Through asking questions, we speak out.

*

In one of my favourite poems of all time, Jameson Fitzpatrick writes:

"I thought I could become a writer
and it was political that I could imagine it"

Writing this collection involved embracing the things I have inherited from my (grand)mothers, and also embracing the privileges that create a vast gulf between my experiences and theirs, and the experiences of the large majority of women living in the world today.

It is a privilege to have imagined this book into being, to have had the freedoms, the tools, the resources to do so.

*

To all the women silenced and suffocated by relationships, families, destinies, this book is for you.

To those exiled from "society" for speaking their minds, and to those who suffer by "society" for never speaking it, this book is for you.

To the girls pulled out of school, and the girls pulled out of their mother's wombs, this book is for you.

To all the people who grow up not fitting the roles, requirements, duties of their genders, and to those who are compelled to resist against them, this book is for you.

To all the warrior writers who came before me and alerted me to the possibilities of language to make social change, this book is for you.

*

Our names give us away.

My name, Ankita, means “someone who leaves a mark”. My mother likes to remind me of this time and again. “I am tired of holding you” she says to us, *“go make something / of your lives”.*

To my extraordinary mother, who gives me oceans for dinner, who gives me the world –

> Here is me making something.
> Here is my mark.

This book, each and every word, is for you.

Mother | Line

Anti-Manifesto

after Zeina Hashem Beck

Stop writing about women.
Stop writing about breasts and motherhood.
Stop writing about rage and trauma and decades of migrations.
Stop telling the story of how your ancestors barricaded their bodies with glass.
Stop writing about girls who marry at dawn and are raped by midday.
Stop finding dimensions to silence.

Stop writing about the ritual
of prayer; the endlessness of hollow chants.
I'm tired of your daily rants. I'm tired of this bare-chested
verse: this poem stripped even of its line.
Just write some love so I can reminisce.

So I wrote him blank verse.
I gave him a lake for a child.
I poured him a sea on a shallow bank.
I cancelled out darkness so eyes had nothing to fear.
I extinguished his mother even.

Then he found he himself was unformed:
not human anymore, nor animate.
Not even a word.

"Women are a bowl, they gather things"
Nesrine Malik

Mother | Line (1)

On your first meeting he tells you to open your palms.
He finds knuckles like eddies, fingers like mangroves.
Funny hands, which will serve as spoon, clutch and whip.

Soft hands, which will stroke and bruise easily.
Harsh hands you fix in fights, as if the loosening
of one hinge will collapse your entire frame.

In your happy place, you are fed with the fingers you eat with.
In your sad place, they freeze like fried pakora.
You're afraid of hands creasing like sheets

under throws. You're afraid of hands shaking like Taiwan.
Their lines tell life like the morning paper, which reminds
each day of mortality: like a child too big to carry

with madness that is inconsolable, that will crumple;
stories so distorted now, pages so mixed up.
You hold the moon in your hands each year.

You're afraid it will give more secrets than you want it to.
I am tired of holding you, you say, *go make something
of your lives.* Nails, the curve of some women, the ache

of morning stiffness. As the truth lands, we arrive in hands
as sudden and seasonal as rainwater after a drought,
to be cupped and cleansed, to be nourished and endured.

Nani (1)

Your body is solid
and folded, your neck is tense with carvings
and cravings.

You've spent forty years grating sugar
in his chai, pouring
eye drops into his sight, arranging

weekday pills in Tupperware,
and on his tongue.

You've got a plait down to your hips,
skin uncharred as a slate tomb.

A preference for soldiers
over doctors, ice-cream
over rotis.

I watch you fan him cool, press his temples
with your index and thumb.

When I hug you, some part of you
dissolves, like sugar
in his tea.

Golden

Ma tells us: never turn a cheek, weakness
    will not be rewarded. The real
world is cruel; they made coolies

of us and they'll do it again if we
    are not careful. When history is left
to be written by the rulers, our school

is our Ma's tongue, Nani's weeping
    fingers. They will catch us lurking
in their boardrooms, the late arrivals,

who should be making weak
    tea. They will interrupt, strike
us off the table, turn the talk straight

back to where they were before we
    walked in, refusing to be silenced, singing
our worth, truthful in the face of sin.

They will call us incapable, weak-
    blooded, all our defences thin
and feeble, before they even let us begin.

Ma tells us, do not be disheartened – we
    are daughters of Kali: bold as gold
and joyful, laughing from January 'til June

when the first rains sing and we
    are close enough to dignity to die
knowing the good ones will be born again.

Goldin's Box

Alia, you liquefy to fit any hospital bed: labour is the trick of sawing bodies
in half, motherhood the trick of the rabbit in the hat. How many rabbits
did it take to convince your husband you were worthwhile?
In the two-storey house you are thin enough to bend into
hidings in the wall:
fold like underwear
into suitcases. Outside
you're bolder
in routines.
Vigilance –
the motto learnt
in a playground
prank. Magic, the way you strut out
unbruised: not a single colour displayed.
To everyone else, it seems like a play of luck,
that in another world, on any other day, you'd emerge
snapped in two. They applause even, as you stand by his side:
harmony another word for victory, good show, another word for lie,
miracle for marriage, another woman tested to the ends of her flexibility.

Nani (2)

O Nani, where are you looking in that red sari, gone brown
through the slippage of paint left out: rusty apple coloured?

Queens in our English art galleries don't look down.
His gaze preens like that peacock in the Jaipur mess

commanding salute, hand hoisted as if already patting
the white boys' heads in Merton Park calling them Son.

How do you do, Son? Tell me, which way is the Metro station?
Why don't you bring a girl close to your chest and call her daughter?

O Nani, won't you tell me you loved? Tell me you loved equally.
Tell me, there were no burnt rotis on your dinner plate?

I wish you'd open your mouth so I could examine the state
of your teeth. I wonder if his lips still smell of betel leaf.

A picture like this with eyes off-gaze, mouths out of touch
would be the third, fourth, or fifth they'd take and we, later discard.

O Nani, where has your teenage smile gone?
Where will mine go? Where will I look on my wedding day?

How to Dismantle a Home

Rip the hooks from the curtains.
The window undresses so easily, so oblivious to shame.
Switch off the heating. Cut off the mains.
The wooden floors will harden. The stove tops will cool.
At once, the air will darken.
Bend each antenna like a spoon, or a back. Muffle the radio,
shroud the television in a white sheet.
Create an out of office email. Stuff the post-box so it doesn't scream.
Dislocate the home, turn the numbers on the door upside down.
Remove the street sign, the other doors won't mind.
Melt the diamond ring. Blow up the roof.
Take a picture of the gaping hole
of a home from above and tweet it widely.
Lock the picture in a cage alongside all the other homes.
Say *We have a problem here. So many illegal homes.*
Say *Look what happened to this poor home because it wasn't careful.*

Say – *Look what happened to this poor woman because she wasn't careful.*
Say – *We have a problem here. So many illegal women.*
Lock her picture in a cage alongside all the other women.
Take a picture of the gaping hole
of a woman from above. Tweet it widely.
Blow up her face. Melt her diamond ring.
The other women won't mind. Remove her name even.
Turn the letters on her birth certificate upside down.
Stuff her mother so she doesn't scream.
Create an out of office email. Shroud her Instagram in a white square.
Muffle her father. Bend each sister like a spoon, or a back.
At once, the air will darken.
The stove tops will cool. The wooden floors will harden.
The mains will cut off. The heating will switch off.
So oblivious to shame, the window undresses so easily.
The curtains rip. Their hooks.

Walking to Agra, Azamgarh, Aligarh, Lucknow

after Arundhati Roy

Stay at home – they say
as if home is a body everyone can retreat to immediately,
a body that is whole and loved and full

Stay at home – they say
as if bus lines have not dried up already
leaving seats raging, empty

Stay at home – they say
as if home is where we are already,
as if home is where we can be

So we walk: drain water flooding
roads; pressurised pipes bursting, choking cities
on things they never wished to see up close

Hand to mouth, now foot to foot
cramping, blistering, holding onto breath
as much as we can – for this air

is all we own – this air all we have
to ourselves, that which will move
as quickly as we clutch it –

Stay at home – they say
and pray – as if all have equal access to God,
as if God is not looking for an easy way out

So, we become endless, turn bodies to diyas –
this way at least the politicians will see us,
the satellites will see us, living women at the stake

Trees catching flame from one another,
blazing, erupting and then, come August,
slowly dying out

Lost Property on Goldhawk Road

It's nothing new: man follows woman home,
she's found dead the next day on a forest floor.
This man is not the first to don a badge,
years before there was one on Goldhawk Road,
saw me in my bright, stripy hat and bow
looking for something lost at a bus depot –
Babe, where you going? See, I work here, look
at my uniform. Lost property? Yeah, that's just below
the stairs, let me take you –
Luckily, I have learnt when to say
I have to go, my dad is just across the road –
turning to where traffic turns red to green,
now, a decade later, wondering where
I could have gone and what I could have been
          had I followed –
                    lost, property, road?

Nani (3)

Nani, where have you hidden your gold?
Within the green gates of locked *almaris?*
Or underneath your bed's wooden frame?
Hanging between your breasts, dropping closer
to your heart than anyone has ever been.
Or upholding your ears like scaffolding –
for they have dismantled so much from
what they have heard, they have drooped in pity.
Maybe in the cavities of forgone teeth:
your own holy grills. Gold like an old
lightbulb, long shadow – sparkling.

Nani, where have you hidden your soul?
Within the green gates of locked *almaris?*
Or underneath your body's wooden frame?
Hanging between your breasts, which drop closer
to your heart than anyone has ever been,
or holding your ears like gentle scaffolding
from all they have heard. Maybe
in the hollow of your mouth: in the holy
words you speak. Gold like an old
lightbulb, long shadow, sparkling.

Ghazal to my Other Tongues

1)

Not my mother, nor my heart, Angrez.
Just the muffled medium of my art, Angrez.

You, child of stubborn parents, you migrant:
If they ask, don't confess. Say you're part Angrez.

Nana says: to fight in languages not ours is be-wakoof!
What vocabularies can justify this lent Angrez?

Where the histories begin and time, even patriots will forgive.
For all who's rich and destined smart's Angrez.

What's your luck? You, who meant "to mark this world"
Cannot shake this word, must depart Angrez.

2)

O modulated Persian, daughter of Arabic, اردو
Sister of Kashmiri, Punjabi and Pashto, اردو

O mirror, who flirts like a thief and lies like a poet,
Who treks across mountains only to announce itself in war: اردو

O nomad of Delhi, mongrel of the north,
Eavesdropper on the local rail from Lucknow to Lahore, اردو

O Hindustani and Afghani, O Pakistani,
O curly-haired worshipper, who writes of God in gold: اردو

O Shayri, O Ghazal, O wandering Nazm –
Give me a voice to translate; a throat to restore اردو

Okra

In English, you are *Ladies' Fingers*:
        bulging with grease, shovelled up lips.

In Igbo you are christened *okuru*:
        frigid and flocculent, measured like gold.

In Arabic you become *bamya*:
        slow-broiled with meat or metaphor.

In Hindi, you're *bhindi*:
        nest of vermin and snake-skinned,
        fried shallow or fragrant with scalloped edges.

We, the soothsayers: from Ghana and Guyana,
        Whitechapel and Wembley

free you from your sins, leaven our hardened
        fingers to spit and slobber

till you are re-born: holier, pliant, tender.

Nani (4)

My grandmother tosses crumbs to the ducks.
Something to do. Someone to feed.
Suddenly her world fills – *look*, she points:

their flurry of snow, their beaks.
Dipped in tea, bread turns to the consistency
of wet sand. Good option, without teeth.

Burnt it again – how quickly the mind
brittles, chars with such stubbornness
that the world feels suddenly unbearable.

Sandwiches – the last thing she forgets to make.
How simple it was, layering toast, braiding
hair, finding the right holes for fingers

in gloves. So often, two fingers bulge in one.
So often, she forgets she has a thumb.

How to Make an Animation

shrink the eagle's back
so over time she turns away

draw each portrait twice
changing one thing at a time

the sun that was there then
will creep lower in the sky

your grandmother will remember
things she has forgotten one at a time:

a receipt, a kitchen light, half
a spoon of sugar

and like that, her tea is just
too bitter

stack up the frames, each only slightly
changed, but the last so different

from the first that even the eagle
forgets her way back

Becoming an Owl

after Safia Elhillo

Paki baat hain	It has been decided in the sweat of their palms or it has ripened
Muh mitha karna	Something to sweeten the dentures, or some good news
Ulu banadiya	Memory entangles her in a spool, makes an owl of her, or a fool
Nani yaad aa jayegi	You will be troubled so hard, they say, you will think of your grandmother
Kala pani	Above the brain is black water, *kala pani* – this is where the exiled go

Nani (5)

Nani says: *when you hiccup it means someone is thinking of you.*
I say, when her stomach burns, she is thinking of someplace else.

The rocks here have no flavour, nor the honey hives or apple trees.
I clap her hands each day to activate her joints.

We breathe in one nostril at a time. *How can those Angrez*
do this without longing; with disinterested elegance?

We do this as worship – listen to the sounds of our bodies,
the way you would listen to the sea. We call this *Reki.*

Here, we bathe in hard water – the water we drink makes us
more hungry. Even the goats are a different flesh. Even –

the potato root. How big the rats are and the squirrels!
How crowded the vaccine centres with volunteers...

So much free time, these people. In Star Bazaar, a man
is employed to bag our things. So much free blood, our people.

Even the Christians pray differently. Our Joseph fasts
for his mother each year. These Johns only give up chocolate for lent.

They pause after each prayer as if scared of offending God.
There is no word in English for this – only a German gesture

towards ache, only a tug-of-war with self: a bland renunciation.
What heroic act must birds perform to be reborn human?

Maybe it is only finding their way home? Maybe each of us
was a bird in a past life – carrying sticks in bated breath.

Nani, when your stomach is burning, is it memory or grief?
Is it your sister's fever you think of, or the freedom of wild fields?

"Can the self survive a partition? If they split your mind in two, which one would be you?"

Rhiya Pau

Mother | Line (2)

Because they scored a blood line up
our mother's spine and because you terra-cotta cup

your hands when you pray and because my father
turned yours out before he left her

and because you call your auntie *khala* not *mausi*
and because your brother blames me

and because we were never in the same relay
race in sports day and because my Nani tries

to hide the burn tears in her bed sheet and because
it took them two years to process

your visit visa and because our mother's
dead now, you are not my sister.

Notes at The Migration Museum

1) *Me | Prim | Prime | Shit | Brit*

In the Atlas, next to the diagrams of tides,
seasons and astronomy, are pie charts
of the British empire
cut by area
by population
by racial constituency.

Dravidians are split from Negros, Afghans from Persians,
Malays from Polynesians.

How many ways could there be to split empire?
To cut British?

2) *Immigrant. Emigrant. Expat. Repat.*

Mother splits us by religion, religion
by caste, caste by gender, gender
by birthright, birthright by education,
education by belief, belief
by politics, politics by age,
age by displacement.

3) *Asylum Seeker. Seasonal Worker. Refugee.*

The first experiment I remember, I lie Mother
in a bath and see how much water
spills out.

Is it better to be heavy, or to be light?
To remain or to overflow?

I cannot contain Mother
or my tongue
or the truth.

It is after all only the curvature
of Mother's tongue which is a certain fact,

that is to say – the boomerang bend of the world which will stretch out
as far as it can contain before invariably
pulling you back.

4) *Newcomer. Traveller. Adventurer.*

Watch me fly among stones
watch me leap
watch me crawl in the rain-soaked grass

Watch me wear many names, like mountain
or wind
or shadow in اردو

and think myself, at any moment in time: invincible.

On Jubilee Weekend, in Ramsgate

this year the Brits have decided to stop working |
four days off | twice within a month | no language
for this besides Christmas | this year it's not even
Jesus but the Queen | the closest thing they have
to Mother Teresa without a cult following or healing |
the same fixation with hands | forgiveness | I have
seen so many dogs piss on cracked fences | blonde
neighbours taking selfies | walking in Kent is like
being in America | all the Union Jacks bunting
the edges of low-lying semi-detached windows |
the greatest Wetherspoons in Great Britain serves
bland burgers overlooking ocean | this is not the
kind of country pride we are used to | standing
orange white and blue on *pandra August* | finding
an embassy or big garden with flag pole | chanting
Bengali poetry like prayer with our people | we |
with ghazal tongues and moon howls | with homes
like boats | which wobble but fill fast with future
ambition do not get this pride | this royalty | but
do not reject it either | instead we too stop working |
we too build strange trifles and subconsciously mouth
the words to *Sweet Caroline* swaying under gulls
who float without flying | for queen and country

Privilege (1)

Never have I ever seen a coup,
performed a bomb drill in school.

I do not look at the sky expecting bullets,
I do not look at the sky expecting floods.

I am from a mild climate –
a family only displaced by choice,

too far west to be partitioned
too far east to be partitioned twice.

In school, they ask us to find letters
our grandparents wrote from war,

I ask them *what war* for my grandfather
has only ever built site plans

for civilian buildings in army messes,
he has only ever been to the stills

of Ladakh and found *Sri* – which is to say
Lakshmi, which is to say, blessing.

There is a violence we carry
but it does not growl like a machine gun

or burst like a firework.
We too are strangers in this narrative

and yet my brothers are turned warriors,
my sisters, daughters of exiled fathers.

Never have I been to a refugee camp
in Bangladesh or hidden

in a neighbour's house in Baghdad.
There are many shades of brown

and I am a privileged one –
remember this, when you pity me:

I, too, have never tasted the rage
of true grief.

I, too, have never watched my country
blow apart.

Kashmir

If there is paradise on earth, this is not she.
Paradise is not scared to announce itself in public.
Paradise is not confined by hours of the day or night.
Paradise is not one man's daughter, another's crime scene.
Jammu, if you were paradise, the plains would sugar themselves
in gold dust, the valleys would line their contours with kohl.
She'd be God and not the victim of believers, and not
the fantasy. She'd be fire and not the sacrificial
goat. Paradise would not hide in barks.
Paradise would say her own name.
She'd spread herself like an azure courtyard.
She'd make a rainbow for sky birds not a burial ground
for scavengers. Kashmir, if you were paradise, the Himalayas
would lie down on earth like Sita. The borders would scrub themselves
away. The bombs would deflect. The horses would bray
and burst into ten-thousand fractals of red.
The buffalos would stop in their tracks.
One billion eyes wouldn't blink today, for having watched
her slip so soon: this paradise on earth, this angel.

Schoolboys

I

Brother imagines himself marching to Burma.
Superman's knickers. A red turban.
Wants to be a hero. He returns with hair
stiff from sweat, cheeks
a freshly punched knuckle hue,
goosebumps.
It's too cold outside
for shorts Mother screams,
scratching nails on stains, draping
a towel around his waist which he sports like a lungi.
Each year, he hoards his uniform: white
shirt, black shoes and always shorts:
cargo shorts, crease resistant, stain
resistant cargo shorts.
When Brother leaves home for good,
Mother packs trousers instead:
mud coloured, stretched
like moth wings on train lights.
Brother wears
them each evening now
as dusk strikes. Knees lunged, ready
for the catch, he raises his arms
and claps.
Mother, he prays, hoping she will hear him:
Bharat Mata Ki Jai.

II

When the wars die out and the soldiers settle
down to simpler lives,
the gunshots will always be wailing
at dawn, the fleeing birds
always whistling,
he will always be craving
after dates and kulfi
as months dry out
like winter knees
and days are feeble pulley
boats on waters
that will soon be bridged.
When the borders fade
like burn-maps on bone,
painful to tread on
and more painful to remove –
the anthem will always
be ready at the lips' tight
gates like guilty schoolboys
chanting *jhanda ooncha*
rahe hamare – even when
the flags are folded
bedsheets and the past skies
have exhaled their rain
and moved on.

Privilege (2)

Caecilius est in horto	*Caecilius is in the garden*
Caecilius in horto sedet	*Caecilius is in the garden sitting*
Servus est in atrio	*The slave is in the atrium*
Servus in atrio laborat	*The slave is in the atrium working*

Cambridge Latin Course, Unit 1

My friends have beautiful gardens: fathers and mothers who sit in it, leisurely.
My friends have gardens with fruit trees, patio flooring, barbecue sets.
My friends have multiple houses with multiple gardens.
My friends have gardeners working, fathers who are bankers, sitting.

To be powerful is to be sitting, while someone else is working.
To be powerful is to own something: a name, a space to call 'garden'.

The Latin word for 'power' is 'imperium'.
The Latin word for 'empire' is 'imperium'.

In India, we have maids who work (verb), with no work (noun), legally speaking.
In India, we have a garden with a swing, laundry rails which carry breeze in clothes.
In India, we have maids who hang clothes, while we are in the garden, sitting.

In private school, we take Latin lessons from Years 7 to 11.
In private school, we venture to Caecilius' de-mosaiced atrium.

The Latin word for 'power' is 'imperium'.
The Latin word for 'empire' is 'imperium '.

Tell me, does 'private' come from 'privus', meaning separate, individual?
Or instead from 'privilegium'?

It's Late and our Mamas don't Know

O friends with the musical tastes of young teenagers! O clean friends and friends as battered as KFC counters, I will always love you louder than the street's glaring darkness! O friends, who paint the world and themselves in glittery yellow and friends who paint it purple like the tide at night, I will love you even when your moods ringlet like pine cones, even when your eyes turn into / onto toilet bowls and your face becomes a flurry of rain! O friends from Chicago and Cairo and friends from Leeds, I've written poems in my dreams with the words you have taught me, I've worn your scent like a life-jacket across years of migrations. O friends who have dared and friends who are too scared to look over the edge because life / height makes them so sick, friends who call and friends who don't – I will never be afraid of double messaging because I have sat in silence next to you too many times to feel awkward! I want to march with you, there is no-one more capable of squashing spiders or the patriarchy. O friends on pills and friends with broken bones and friends I should have spoken to more, I wish your trauma away! I never want anyone to look at you in a way that is not for respect or adoration. O happy babies! O ignorant angels! O fierce soldiers in violet saris and gold nose-rings, I want to frame your faces in Vogue and buy you Chanel and clothe all your decisions in choice! I want to dance with you even when it's late and our mamas don't know.

Baba Ghanoush

My love likes her vine leaves stuffed with rice:
saffron-infused, cardamom-infused rice.
She likes her cucumbers lined with salt,
which reminds her of her father's sleepy
fishing town and those distant Middle-Eastern
trees. My love makes me okra in a thick,
tomato stew, so different to ours,
yet close enough to remind me of home.
Friendship is *Baba Ghanoush* in our lunch
boxes: the pulp of a whole aubergine
soaking like a child in summer sun until
the skin is brown, soft and impressionable.

Adulthood is finding the right combination
of heat and olive oil to allow the meaty
fruit to crush in the teeth. This is the way
we carve our first home: bringing as many
splints as we can from separate childhoods,
gathering new ones from the aisles. My heart
gives me Egypt in a spoonful of Za'atar
and I give her immigrant Britain
in a splutter of cumin. Mothers linger
on the sides, hearing us become them;
our routines only theirs to thank for, our spices,
our blends and even our greedy tongues.

Privilege (3)

Delhi, this city of 29 million people
only has ventilators on 100 beds.

In other news, Aldi tweets
"Can Colin and Cuthbert be friends?"

In Wales, they have legalised
the kwytch; in France, criminalised

the hijab, made it legal to ****
without consent. I am now so scared

of simple things: a breath of fresh air
while I run, a cough at the back

of a carriage, its stifling permanence.
I am scared of hugging my best

friend – of what I could give her
and how much of her will stick.

In the absence of touch, I learn
the body of the city: the way

she slopes into the river's basin
swatting off responsibility –

a tired mother. Lorries scurry up
her thighs: last night's bruises drain

into gutters. The tantrums of trees
meet with the steady sweeping

of daily soldiers. My body has aged
two years. The frown lines

have made a visible track.
I am scared of all this: of living

so freely, knowing someone else's
future is constantly under attack.

Love(less)

I am in a loveless marriage. He is making Paneer Tikka Masala.
In the school parking lot, I am talking like my mother.
He has taken me to an American diner where we are drinking from jars.
He is singing. Something by Bruno Mars.
I am hiding in the toilet. There are brown stains on the roof.
The doctor has pushed me on a bed the size of a bread loaf.
He is asking me, and Mum is asking me, *What is the problem?*
We could be anywhere in the world. Hawaii. Canada. Lebanon.
He has lost the hair on his head fighting with my mother.
I am in a locked room. He is asking me, *What is the matter?*

What is the matter? Dad is asking me. I have locked myself in a room.
He is fighting with my mother. He has lost the hair on his head.
Hawaii. Canada. Lebanon. We could go anywhere in the world.
What is the problem? Mum is asking me. He is asking me.
I am the size of a bread loaf; the nurse has pushed me on a bed.
There are brown stains on the roof of the toilet I am hiding in.
He is singing something by Bruno Mars.
We are drinking from jars like Americans in London.
I am in the school parking lot. I have lost my mother
in a loveless marriage making Paneer Tikka Masala.

Brown Mums

how they always stuck together: the brown mums in the school parking
lot | on day one I ask you to be my friend | invent a handshake | clap

your skin to test it's firm | the white mums come in packs | all skinny
jeans and stuck-up scarves | our mums become friends | *of course they do*

(green eyes seem to imply behind dark shades | hair straight like fresh
road) | in break time we trade words our mums taught us like stickers

or cheesestrings | *why can't they say things the right way?* Isobel says
or was it Daisy | lemon drizzle cake hair | already little women in leggings

and crop tops | all freckles and friends | we're stuck in the changing rooms
scared to take our clothes off | show our loud, white vests and brown

stomachs | bellybuttons tucked in | *always the last in class* your mum says or
was it mine? | dried Pritt stuck on thumbs | *tell me what you learned today*

Night Vigil

Didi gets the bottom bunk and you get the top –
you are uncomfortable or you are ecstatic.

You wake up in a shared dream,
separate bodies hot and bothered.

Everything is safe. The wind is blowing.
You will stumble into Didi's bed –

troubled warrior, begging for stories.
There will be fighting next door, or ****

In the single that borders their double, you hear
them throwing things across the room.

You and Didi will jam your ears against the wall,
bodies bunched together like frozen spinach.

You are cold and this is not difficult.
In the next dream, there will be strangers

in the house – you will slide out from a slip
in the door like a cat, leave child-like, angelic.

When the night is too dark to understand
you hug until her stomach hurts,

say, with the squeaky voice you conjure for pity
take me down the corridor please

until you appear, a wedge between their legs
just small enough to push them apart.

Privilege (4)

Cambridge Latin Course, Unit 1 – *"In Trinclinio"*

I

Grumio enters the dining room.
Grumio is carrying the peacock.

Clemens enters the dining room.
Clemens is carrying wine.

Caecilius tastes the peacock.
"The peacock is very good!" shouts Caecilius.

The merchant also tastes the peacock.
The merchant praises the dinner.

The master praises the cook.
Grumio goes out.

A slave-girl enters.
The slave-girl sings sweetly.

The slave-girl pleases the master.
The slave-girl pleases the merchant.

Soon the master is sleeping.
The friend is also sleeping.

Grumio enters the kitchen and looks around.
The cook sees the food on the table.

Grumio eats the food and drinks the wine.
Caecilius does not see Grumio.

The cook feasts like a king in the dining room.
The cook sees the slave-girl.

The slave-girl pleases Grumio.
Grumio is very happy.

II

Ganesh enters the dining room.
Ganesh is carrying the mutton.

Chandu enters the dining room.
Chandu is carrying whiskey.

Chaacha tastes the mutton.
"The mutton is very good!" shouts Chaacha.

The business man also tastes the mutton.
The business man praises the dinner.

Sir praises the cook.
Ganesh goes out.

The maid's girl enters.
The maid's girl sings sweetly.

The maid's girl pleases Sir.
The maid's girl pleases the business man.

Soon Sir is sleeping.
The business partner is also sleeping.

Ganesh enters the kitchen and looks around.
The cook sees the food on the table.

Ganesh eats the food and drinks the whiskey.
Chaacha does not see Ganesh.

The cook feasts like a king in the dining room.
The cook sees the maid's girl.

The maid's girl pleases Ganesh.
Ganesh is very happy.

To the Date who Asks me what a Poem is

We are on the top of a shallow hill. On our right,
the sinking sun. Behind us, Battersea's four Buddhas.

I say, a poem is about feeling, a unit of text
that in existing in its singular form makes you quiver.

We laugh about how strange this is – *of course*
the white women on yoga mats block our view. This cannot

compare to Thailand, Vietnam, where he's been before.
He says – what if I rip a page out of a novel?

Would that be a poem? Later, we talk of Kashmir –
the state that never made its mind up, the sympathy

of the West, the *Gosh, I feel so sorry for your people.*
Yes, I say, it could be if read that way. He shows me

a drawing of a never-ending spiral: both the inside
and outside of an art gallery like a patient whose guts

are on display. This is the art I like, he says, geometric,
regular. We talk of the complexity of the situation, how

no-one pulled their armies out. I say – a poem relies
on some sort of strategy – within the seams there is craft,

there is the steady march of metre, there is the opportune
placement of a line break. He still doesn't get it. He says –

I don't like art with no rules. He says – obviously,
I don't agree with the internet being cut off. Obviously,

I still believe in freedom of speech. I say, a poem
is the most efficient art form, and with that he pictures

a machine gun. I say – you should read it, I promise.
It has taken me two decades to understand. It has taken

my life. And with that he thanks me for my time.

"Karm Karo, Phal ki Chinta Mat Karo"
Bhagavad Gita

Mother | Line (3)

In the vents of St Paul's
passing on the rumour of God.
they whisper to
altered like words
they must have whispered –
lost to these mosaic
instead like one understands
of a low-lying aeroplane.
goes on – the message
believe in God: this, their
and you will have God
the flap of one ear
to receive the daily baton
looks back on the first.
here where young boys are
too much of themselves, *God*
himself, he must.
spun like prayer beads or
which will stick
or leave like others,
under some spot of dome
despite all, yes,

angels run in relay
Did you hear
the altar pieces – voices
sifted through air. *Did you hear*
what they heard
strangers understood
the tones
Did you hear, the tale
passes on,
mother's promise
on your side,
always turning upwards
the way each line of poetry
Yes, even
scared to confess
will reveal
And this, which may be
recited in psalms,
like certain fathers
in some certain light
believed
still believed.

Stray Dogs

I

On Raju's walk home from school every evening
the stray dogs taunt him: brown furs clenched around
their waists like tight belts, ribs jutting out –

He learns to fear them, believing his mother's stories,
how Shalja Aunty's son got rabies from the clutch of one –

Soon, he becomes so afraid, he starts to run,
past the stationery shack, the dusty cricket field.

The quicker he runs, the quicker he can reach
the steel gates of the bungalow on the second left in Sector C,
leave behind their hungry smiles, spiny legs like battoned mobs!

The quicker he runs, the more his eyes latch on newspaper
stories that mention dogs of any kind – mongrels left to scavenge
on garbage or groomed dogs turned savage.

Even in another country he recognises those tormentors
in the eyes of every dog on the street, thinks to himself –
dogs will be dogs, it's in their blood, in their genes.

II

On Sweety's walk home from school every evening
the stray boys taunt her: brown hands clenched around
their waists like tight belts, ribs jutting out –

She learns to fear them – believing her mother's stories,
how Shalja Aunty's daughter got pregnant from the clutch of one –

Soon, she becomes so afraid, she starts to run –
past the stationery shack, the dusty cricket field.

The quicker she runs, the quicker she can reach
the steel gates of the bungalow on the second left in Sector C,
leave behind their hungry smiles, spiny legs like battoned mobs!

The quicker she runs, the more her eyes stray on newspaper
stories that mention boys of any kind: teenage boys left to feed
on garbage or groomed men turned savage.

Even in another country she recognises those tormentors
in the eyes of every boy on the street, thinks to herself –
boys will be boys, it's in their blood, in their genes.

Mother(less) | | or | | The Five Stages of Grief

1.

All she wanted was a new dress that time there was a hole in her navel
that turned her into an astronaut, half life-less.

The bleeding hadn't stopped. He stuffed her with thick pulp
through a plastic tube, rolled her in prayer.

She refused to speak: hair short and sleeked
back, compressed curls tight to the scalp, hard like a helmet.

Next time, he vouched, I will not make the same mistake. She'll leave
in a brand new designer piece, high on a chariot surrounded by her people.

I'll place one palm on her forehead, the other on her lower neck:
she likes the smallness of them there, the warmth. Careful

not to let her slip too soon, I'll lift the bare back I've only known
through pain, let the drooping breasts rest on my own chest.

I'll drop a white, silk gown over her neck, tugging tight over legs
scraggly with weight. Then, lay her down again.

I will not bury her tonight. No, I will raise her up, carry her
in a funeral pyre and watch as her new dress goes up in flames.

I will share her then, speck by speck, with the tongue of the Ganga.
Generations will bathe in remnants of my mother.

2.

do not hesitate in the passing of salt

continue the ritual of observing the oak cabinet
full of empty, gleaming glasses, the occasional crystal animal

hear them deepen their voice – the way women
do when they want to sound lion

when you are done eating, walk steadily to the kitchen sink, breathe unremarkably

(behind you, their eyes will writhe – they have
never hated a man's back as much as this)

turn on the tap – it makes no dramatic dents on the lashes
of food: bright sauce turned clot red, crumbs stuck
on the plate until they sag and depart

pick up a dry sponge – swaddle it until the plate
sparkles like a lake you could drown in

turn off the tap, turn around, face the family
who is now standing in the doorway, filling it like a jug of water

find a fruit in the fruit bowl to contemplate – think of breaking
the bowl, squeezing an apple core in your fists until all the seeds emerge

think of the skin of a banana: how flimsy it is to knot
stand by the window – wait for volume to return, to make yourself acceptable

3.

The last time he said goodbye
it was hastily scribbled with whiteboard pen

Dada had stopped using his words, ears of wax,
diabetic heart a little too sweet for sorrow

It's easier this way he wrote, handing him the pen,
rubbing off words as he read them

Dadi, who could barely speak by then,
murmured prayers she once recited before bed

as if *shaanti* would bring back his body
of no hair, his sometimes vacant voice

When all that needs to be done is done
the space between him and them is shaanti

There is no hurrying from prayer to prayer
for they are shaanti

Eyes stare blankly at the wall,
at the remaining moths, for the wall is shaanti

The Hindi word for peace is quiet:
as if his throat is not already a dry well

as if silence is not the easiest way
to cut someone off

4.

Int.

Dad enters in a faded polo neck,
hands in his pockets, heavy
metal in headphones, brown shoes,
black jacket, half-grey head.
Mum – *Do you want some water?*

Ext.

Dad cusses in bus to Waterloo.
This bus is on diversion. Bottle neck.

Flashback.

His mother, wise eyed, grey head,
body slumped on nurse's bed. Heavy.

Int.

Dad takes off his shoes.

Put yourself in my shoes
for once – Dad to Mum draining water,
dropping bags of shopping, heavy.

Flashback.

His mother grasps a dream. Stretches neck.
Dad rushes to his bed. Catches her head.

Flashback.

Temple. Topless pundit blesses Dad's head.
Dad takes off his shoes.
Motherless, father rips the beads off his neck,
wrings free from holy water,
thinks of mother as ash, heavy.

Ext.

Bus stops. Clouds: grey/white and heavy.
Dad walks home with hand over head.
His mother appears everywhere like water
collecting on his coat, his bags, his shoes.

Int.

I am trying, LISTEN to me – Mum clutching Dad's neck.

End.

Dad holds his head heavy in a polo-neck,
sinks into Mum like shoes in water.

5.

Every day we find new ways to forgive.
Turn off the television for days to forgive.

Our tongue lost in knots only we can undo –
Isn't it better than running away to forgive?

Pain is like rage is like empty desire:
learn how our ancestors prayed to forgive.

Tape up the doors, split memories like halwa –
nest hearts on knees and sway to forgive.

What's lost can't be mended. How, the dead?
Dab paint on these scenes of grey to forgive.

But time is not cyclical – this, too, will fade:
Raju – says Mummy – yesterday will forgive.

Experiments in Faith

Raju rolls a Raagi roti, hands a mother's yellow
as he swills shallow dough, red-onion, grated carrot.

On Hosur Road at noon, the coconut seller piles
his bicycle high like a donkey's back.

"Take a spoonful of chyawanprash" the doctor says on TV,
sticky like polish on steel chammach or stirred into hot dhoodh.
This will give you double immunity: God-food."

Dadi chops ginger on her palm, raw skin on the knife's downbow.
It could, in the slight gamble of a second, slip and screech.
But it never will, she says, who has played
with knives all her life.

All I ask is this: four coconuts please:
two to drink, and two to eat.

Twice a month, we perch
on the edges of reason while the floors thin to tight-rope.
We walk, afraid of releasing breath, afraid of rain-cracked ceilings.

One for ten rupees, the coconut seller chants to the smog
and the sirens while the potholes bloat with yesterday's rain.

Years later, we look up the ingredients:
honey and sugar, amla and cinnamon bark
sandalwood, ghee, rose chestnuts and tiger's claw.

Twice a year, we forget how many teeth we have
and where the pain is in our gums.

He extends his butcher's saw and makes clean cuts
on the street's jagged teeth. *Here you go,* he says:
two to drink and two to eat.

The food of the gods no less than a spice plantation,
the essence of the worlds' trees: this, our legacy,

Where will you go next Uncle Ji?
Will you go to Adugodi, or Marathalli?

There is the joy of watching a moment suspend: tilt one way
and then another, as if to say – bear with me,
stay with me, while I make my decision.

Oh mother of these hanging cattle! Fisherman
of these palms! Where will you go next carrying your day's catch
on your back, while the streets spill as if made of grapefruit?

Papa rolls a Raagi roti, hands a mother's yellow.
He does not know if today's flame will be kind
but in this moment, fool for love,
he is faithful.

Sky Burial

When the pilot shut his cockpit, did he leave
any debris? A lobe of chewing gum perhaps? A *Times*
crossword with the 'up' incomplete?

I've heard in Tibet and Mongolia, the dead are left
out in the open, laid bare by birds of prey: fleshy
scarecrows evaporating in a mountain's breath.

The Zoroastrians build open-roofed towers instead;
hushed and pure-blooded they wait for bones to erode in scraps
of sunlight, to decompose like Happy Princes.

Over the ocean, limbs turn to stale soda;
the pilot folds the bodies into brace, buckles them to soul.
Only these are truly airborne.

Years later feathers from another plane's burnt wing
float like driftwood under wide tides: the footprint
of a tyre, a flap on a sandbank,

letters found jumbled on mouths
waiting for the miracles to stack up
and produce another arrival.

On Duty

Because Krishna tells Arjun do your work and you will do your duty.
Because Bapu says – even a grain of salt can prove your duty.

Because the teacher rides alone from Chandigarh to Jaipur
and there is always a lamp to study under in the school of duty.

Because in the thick of night the soldiers fight for "heaven on earth"
and Arjun surrenders his brothers for the love of duty.

Because Blake finds heaven so easy, and mother finds marriage
and grandmother finds that silence is the best fool of duty.

Because it only costs ten cows to kill a woman of any class,
but a hundred for a Vaisya; one thousand for a Kshatriya – the rule of duty.

Because in Kargil, the blast is thick with the faithful's tongues:
Sanskrit, Arabic, Urdu, Hebrew: the choral cues of duty.

Because politicians hand out cannisters of gas and slogans of promise
and say, vote with your mind, and we will fulfil your duty.

Because the poor man fasts without salt and ginger, love and laughter
only to realise there is nothing left to swallow but duty.

Because Krishna opens his mouth and Yashoda sees the world,
she says no harm will come to you, my son, if you do your duty.

"Because you're worth it"
L'Oréal Paris

Mother | Line (4)

For half an hour every three weeks, Mama plasters
her roots with L'Oréal's Number Four or Five from Boots.

She is slicked back like John Travolta from Grease,
head in a cap like Sandy, and then for the week

that proceeds she's Madhuri Dixit dancing on L'Oréal
ads, and the river runs back up the mountain.

Aunty at the parlour tells me my hairs are too unruly,
each grows in its own direction, each has its own will.

In the hot room – we barely speak at all. It is hard
to speak when your skin is burning. Growing up,

I pray for divine intervention. The first item I purchase
is a stick of kajal. I've seen Rani Mukerji

embroider her eyes with a bold underline.
I have seen Kajol become angelic. I dream of weddings

with the whole world dancing, not a happy world
but a truthful one – for that is what my mama taught me

making me drop every coin I found back on the floor,
say things the right way not necessarily the kind way.

After all, it is only shame that comes to haunt you –
the last email you ignore, the way at a sleepover

you say you have another mother: *"just a bit of banter"*
and your world ceases to make sense anymore.

Kajal

What are you afraid of when you say she is beautiful?
That your tongue will be plagiarised, praise turned to cuss?

As she crosses you, you catch her smile peeping from a single
dimpled cheek, you can't help but remark: she is beautiful.

As she drifts into unknown dreams, fingers rolled up,
skin a waft of grey agarbatti, she is beautiful.

But in the morning you are guilty – now you know
what you know, you are afraid she is beautiful.

Her lips will grow like the Calcutta skyline, body
a Bannerghatta tiger, you're afraid she is beautiful.

They will look, eyes the lying moons wives find in trees
through sieves and saris, you're afraid she is beautiful.

Her smile gains the shyness of the first rain in May
and as she catches her face a puddle, she knows she is beautiful.

So you sharpen your kajal: sandalwood pencil
dip-dyed in ghee. It is time now, for they know she's beautiful.

Every day, before you pray, you draw orbs on cheeks
and chin, black spots you colour in to make her less beautiful.

What are you afraid of when you say she is beautiful?
That your tongue will be plagiarised, praise turned to cuss.

Soon you are afraid she will be afraid she is beautiful.
So say now, before it's too late: she is beautiful.

She is beautiful. *She* is beautiful.

Ganesh's Monologue

my parents invoke god in different ways

pita saves his heart for Lakshmi,
prays for a woman who will kneel for him
and bear beautiful children

ma holds the heart of Durga,
she will kneel for no-one but a lion

pita asks for one of her arms at least
to hold at night, to dance with in the haze of dusk

ma gives him an image –
a picture to pose with when the nights
are sea-sick and the days are feverish

pita picks flowers for her hair
but ma wants rivers and mountains

pita gives her his lap
but ma wants his legs

ma wants to run, to run, to run
and have no-one watch her

pita gives her locks for bedroom doors,
ma wants the keys, the keys, the keys

pita accuses her of thinking herself a devi
while posing for a devotee,
ma finds him far away and lonely:

the Ram who doesn't trust Sita
even with a demon, the Ram who must come back
to a palace with no lights

but in the morning, ma builds
a fortress of a child who will crawl
on his lap like Lakshmi, who will glue the chipped

tukras of his soul piece by piece and instead, in his child
he finds Durga – he finds the strength
of an army – he finds Kali

High Tide

Kylie Minogue is in my mother's bedroom.
They're both trying on her clothes.

Mum says – *you'd look elegant in this embroidered sari,*
reaches for her casket of gold.

Kylie laughs, picks out my mum's floor-length gown
instead, the only one she owns. On Minogue,

it trails like a wedding dress. By the mirrors,
they are trying to remove age from their skin, bandaging

their cheeks. Kylie tries on Mum's bright pink lip –
the one she wore last hosting a party for Dad,

daring herself to breathe in a tight, slit skirt,
a burgundy blouse. *How do I look*, she said to Dad,

eyes like a cigarette lighter. Dad looked
at his phone instead, thumb like wobbling jelly.

Downstairs the guests hide behind plant-pots
and sofas, and the table spreads its legs out.

How do you keep yourself so young, Mum asks
Kylie, as she reveals her final look, taping

two dictionaries to her feet for extra height.
I think you know – Kylie sings, chiggy-wigging

out of the bathroom, out of my mother's room,
out of the front door – while Mum

takes a final look at herself in the mirror –
La-la-la, la-la-la-la-la, La-la-la, la-la-la-la-la.

Portrait of Lovers and their Prayers

1)

as if begging for solace
cupping the moon in a steel container
hoping tonight their words would be gentle
like bhajan of Aarti in prayer –
we never understand their curses, only offerings:
backs kneeling against wall,
heads cool on the temple floor,
eyes closed like Shiva, who is after all
more God than destroyer

2)

as if begging for forgiveness
for a crime he never committed
opening his dirty palms for judgement –
fool, who thinks these busy Gods
will be so kind, as if that's how faith
works: one day holding it all,
the next, only yesterday's travel card

3)

there is nothing sacred
about her body, only ashamed –
but maybe one day, after the ashes,
she will excavate a temple
& beneath that a minaret,
& beneath that the water table
still feeding aqueducts of old Rome
& before all of that unbelonging
she will find a raincoat
holding a shameless woman holding the rain

How to Love a Man who Leaves

I

Turn your brain into a reel.
Scroll until the blankets go full circle.

Jump off a wall; the hospital will be there
to pick you up and your bruised heel.

Leave the large Dominos box on the bench facing the set sun and
pour yourself in an egg cup, finding the world goes round and round.

Repeat the dates you've done together differently.
Don't look out until the sky blues and you're waving again from a night bus.

Take pictures of the chopping board and raw mushrooms and dirty plates.
Grow back into the child you were when Mama's lap wasn't safe.

Take pictures of your face in five angles.
Download another dating app. Get bored.

Take pictures of the teenage couple, who hug awkwardly and kiss more so.
Zoom in to feel sorry for yourself.

Take pictures of your shadow so there are two of you.
Demolish pink playdough and twitter. Create new friends.

Watch everything with subtitles.

Blame yourself for the way you come across now,
having not jumped off the wall.

II

One eye gaping, the other a perfectly curled
blinker, mesmerised.

Fear of brown and beautiful eyes.

The topography of the bed like a field
of daisies: shadows, blue-black on the wall.

His hand clenching keys, teeth on your neck.
Mouth open slightly, afraid to speak.

More open than open and then shut.
Fear of the lack of fear.

Call me a sandcastle, malleable, ready to fold
and pack; a dry-cleaned Sunday shirt.

Call me a goldfish; undeserving of gold.
Call me a guilty pleasure.

Call me what I am: a poster girl with pouched-out
lips, two clip-on hoops scrambling for the nib

of a plastic pen hid among tobacco flakes
at the bottom of a large grey bag

hoping he'll call her: anything, anything, anything.

Scenes from the Night Bus

The absence of people make the windows talk.
"We give a fork" one says, as transparent as a lake.
"Don't worry that we're shut" says another,
"just visit our branch around the corner"
(directing to a dump)

The signs on the offices are bold and bordered:
"Hogan Lovells" is
"back open for business".

Buildings now shut still shine:
"Starbucks"
"Café Concerto"
"Clink Hostels"

A bus stop is a temptress – its face
plastered with some stimulant invitations such as:
"Do you want these boots?"

Takeaway slums leave their numbers
"You me, Sushi"
"Delivered to your door".

A hospital, still breathing, points out ER.

The underground gives us a big, red gasp
signing for something else, a route to anywhere
(within time, zone and line).

A flock of zebra crossing balloons maraud
the darkness looking for people to carry.

Loud motorcycles mate in the distance like foxes.

Failures of lonely moths look for spaces
between windows to fly into
and find a flame.

Ode to Butterflies

first crush raced butterfly on the boys' team
        more *dragon* than Monarch
gliding through the water like a chrysalis
        merman with his legs glued shut
never knew if I wanted him or his streamline
        his jet – how he sliced through anything
took it apart, rode a bike with no hands
        gave me butterflies

second crush was strongman, muscles flexed
        as he helped unload boxes
from the van with the *let-me-take-that-off-you*
        look and was it relief or attraction
the passing of what I held onto him
        the *do-you-want-it-here?* sign –
yes-here-there-or-anywhere – voice like butter
        arms that could make me fly

third crush was destined – *if-we-get-married*
        it-would-be-so-typical
aunties waiting in the hall with the plastic chairs
        napkin-white broad-smiled
have-you-met-X's-son-he's-about-your-age
        my eyes watering from being beautiful
like Aishwarya Rai's, your lips buttery
        hands greasy, mine – dry

fourth crush is nearly my boyfriend
          blank-sheeted man I fold like origami
I've read so much into what he's told me
          my mind full of erotic stories
from late night brain reels, I try to find
          patterns in the space between
replies, they're lengthening, dazzling
          short-lived butterflies

          Of course, all the smart ones lie.
fifth is the first to make me cry –
          wet like butter, *bye*.

Ode to the Custard Apple

you think we only eat chaotically	*chicken balti* dripping
skin licking, mouths sticking	but our apples have skins of iguanas
firm and globular	turning day to night in a single fist
clouds for cartilage	stars for knuckles
our mangoes	can be devoured ten different ways
pierced	at the top and held in our hands
like a prayer	or else sliced into fragments:
a poem in epic form	Nana always says
don't talk of anything on the table	so you can appreciate how
the food has been made today	not for takeaway or buffet
but especially for you	the way you like it
Nani measures cups in eyes	she could cook blind
by testing degrees of heat	on the flap of her tongue –
my plate is the earth	from an aeroplane:
my mother gives me oceans	for dinner
mixing sticky lush with spice	full body collapse
with the willpower of tusks	you think we eat chaotically?
chicken balti dripping skin licking	mouths sticking
but each of our fruits	is a wonder of the world

O Ma!

Here, the kids are too quiet! Dogs
sit on beds, religion is an immigration

officer with a language barrier...
You are from a 40-foot album tidied

away, your father's leather-bound address
book with all the homes you've ever

lived in and those out of reach. You stack
your mother's pots by the doorway;

later, these will be fire escapes; later,
you will lock the door. You, the sister

between two brothers skipping stones
down the railway line to Jamshedpur.

You, the rani or rebel climbing ladders
up a petrol tank where you're the only

woman on patrol. You, the dinner date
who never wants marriage until you do,

then, you the young mother balancing
breast milk with books, dancing the tango

down the highway but never speeding,
watching us sleeping on one bed, our big

bodies juxtaposed like our politics,
your father dreaming of the first home

he engineered, your dog sleeping outside,
the sun, a shrine. This is your home, Ma!

We, the Pilgrims

and when you arrive at the waters   they don't disappoint
your breath is loud and greedy   your legs   clockwork

rusty   your eyes have nothing but the grey of road
the occasional secret   of a windy tree

here the sun blends like an immigrant   in a sky
she once owned   she has known what it is to be feared

the cranes salute   the sand is contoured
ships are solitary   moored   bridges peak and fall

like kathak dancers   these static birds charm
these plains still   a page of poetry from above

these mud banks are Ganga   these wide skies
are Kerala   the sun spills like your mother's

sindoor   we, the pilgrims from Hammersmith
and Hounslow   from Vauxhall and Battersea   each carry

the weight of hips   the responsibility of hungry souls
each arrive   eager   expectant   enthralled

A Woman is Laughing

Translation of 'Ek Aurat ki Hansi' – Fahmida Riaz

Under the singing watch
of a rocky mountain
a woman is laughing.
No fame, no money
but bold with the guts
of a free body:
a woman laughing.

In all the world's temples,
you will not hear the lush tremor
of a woman laughing.
In the market of all treasures,
you will not find the baby balm
of a woman laughing.
This rare narcotic she bears
so freely cannot be captive, sold.

Come then, become breeze.
In the wild valley, lapping
her face with kisses –
hair flying long and loose,
wind's daughter is singing
alongside the wind:
a woman is laughing.

NOTES

Golden: This poem takes the form of a golden shovel, devised by American poet Terrance Hayes, in homage to Gwendolyn Brooks. When read in order, the last words or phrases of most of the lines make up the words of Brooks' poem of resistance "We Real Cool":

We Real Cool, Gwendolyn Brooks
The Pool Players.
Seven at the Golden Shovel.

We real cool. We
Left school. We

Lurk late. We
Strike straight. We

Sing sin. We
Thin gin. We

Jazz June. We
Die soon.

Goldin's Box: This title of this poem comes from the famous magician Horace Goldin, who popularised the magic trick of "Sawing through a woman". This magic trick started in World War One to give people hope that bodies can be sown back together again. In 1921, Goldin presented the first version of the trick which looks like the modern day trick.

Walking to Agra, Azamgarh, Aligarh, Lucknow: On March 24th 2020, India announced an overnight lockdown. Millions of migrant workers, who had left their villages or towns to go work in big cities, had to walk back home with no public transport in sight. This was the biggest migration of people across India, since the partition in 1947. In an article for The Financial Times, Arundhati Roy writes:

"They walked for days, towards Badaun, Agra, Azamgarh, Aligarh, Lucknow, Gorakhpur — hundreds of kilometres away. Some died on the way"

Ghazal to my Other Tongues: This is the first of many ghazals in this collection. Originally an Arabic poetic form, this form spread across the Indian subcontinent in the twelfth century, with the Mughal Empire. There are a variety of rules for this form. For one, each couplet should end on the same word or phrase. In this ghazal, I have chosen two words

– “Angrez”, which means English in Hindi, and “اردو”, which means Urdu. Another rule is that the poet’s name or reference to it, should appear in the final couplet. My name means “someone who leaves a mark on this world” – this is what I reference in the final couplet of part one of the ghazal.

Privilege (3): On April 19th 2021, amidst a second wave of COVID turmoil, New Delhi imposed a week-long lockdown. An article at the time said: “This city of 29 million people has fewer than 100 beds with ventilators”. The next day, headlines of London’s daily tabloid paper The Metro, centred around Aldi’s legal battle with Marks and Spencer. The article states: “Marks and Spencer has lodged an intellectual property claim with the High Court, claiming Cuthbert looks far too similar to its Colin the Caterpillar Cake”.

Mother(less) || or || The Five Stages of Grief: The five stages of grief model was introduced by Swiss-American psychiatrist Elisabeth Kubler-Ross in her 1969 book *On Death and Dying*. She originally describes stages to describe the mind-frame of terminally ill patients who come to terms with their own deaths. These stages have since been popularised to describe the process grieving friends and family go through, which seems to be similar. The stages are:

1. Denial
2. Anger
3. Bargaining
4. Depression
5. Acceptance

A Woman is Laughing: *[Reprinted from an introduction to this translation I wrote for Modern Poetry in Translation]*

“Loud, ugly, unashamed and sometimes disrespectful, laughter can be an unexpected form of liberation. We rarely laugh in rooms that do not make us feel welcome. To laugh with someone, truly and not consciously, is to think yourself their equal. In ‘Ek Aurat ki Hansi’, Pakistani poet Fahmida Riaz portrays a woman’s laughter as a sign of her ‘azadi’ (freedom). Like many of our foremothers, Riaz fought for her right to laugh – to laugh at the religious separatism in post-partition India and Pakistan (which she captures in her poem ‘Tum Bilkul Hum Jaise Nikle’) and at the continued suppression of marginalised voices.

Riaz also spent a lot of time honouring her lineage, working on translations of the female Farsi poet Forugh Farrokhzad, as well as Rumi, into Urdu. Despite her often radical gaze, when Riaz passed away in 2018, she was celebrated on both sides of the border as an extraordinary voice of authority. In an interview, Riaz said: ‘I am not an exceptionally politically over-charged poet. Perhaps the only exception is that I am a woman.'

I have grown up with women who laugh. My mother, who starts laughing midway through a story she is trying to tell you. My beautiful best friend, whose laugh emerges first in her eyes, then in the 'lush tremor' of her open mouth, before erupting finally into full-blown ecstasy. My translation is for all the women in my life, who have given, and continue to give me, the permission to laugh."

We are keen to make the experience of reading this collection as dynamic and interactive as possible - access live performance footage of the poems, as well as additional explanatory videos through the YouTube playlist link here:

ACKNOWLEDGEMENTS

Thank you to Mama and Papa for your pride, your love, your trust. I do not know how you have the energy to parent for so long and so well.

Thank you to Nani and Nana, Dadi and Dada, for your wisdom, your language, for raising such a beautiful family.

Thank you to my siblings. To Didi, my queen, my mirror image, and my constant cheerleader. To Desh, my baby, my bubble and my brilliant rock-star – I love you the most in the world. And to my latest sibling, Vishesh, for a future of silliness and sophistication.

Thank you to my friends, who are family. To Iman, my soulmate, for the countless conversations, reflections and experiences that have shaped the ideas in this book. To Zainab, my forever friend and first muse – I am so proud of the person you have become, for your ambition, your passion, and your companionship. And to Rhiya, my "other half", my kindred spirit – for sharing each stage of this journey with me (both literal and metaphorical) over the last three years. Thank you also to Saloni, Vicky, Clem, Lucy, Gordon, Loris, my numerous school, university and work pals, my miracle berries, my supergirls – too many of you are special to name, you inspire me, ground me and bring me joy.

Thank you to The Poetry Society and Foyle Young Poets of the Year Award for giving me tote bags full of poetry, and glorious foam notebooks. And to Sophie Breese, for being the most exceptional of teachers.

Thank you to the Barbican Young Poets Programme for adopting me when I was 16 and turning me into a poet. Thank you especially to Jacob Sam La-Rose, for your tireless vision, precision and continual challenge. Thank you also to Jasmine Cooray and Kayo Chingonyi. To Kareem for making me feel like a champion each time I left stage. To Omar for your friendship and that waffle stick in Camden. To Bobbi and Lana, for your sisterhood. To the extended BYP crew, past and present – who keep appearing, keep achieving and keep bringing me home.

Thank you to the Octavia Poetry Collective, to Rachel Long for your mentorship – so many of these poems felt safe in your magical hands, and to Sarah, Zahrah, Amaal for your friendship.

Thank you to Deborah Frances-White and The Guilty Feminist community, for taking my poetry, and bringing it to the (feminist) masses.

Thank you to ORIGINS, Poets for Partition, Apples and Snakes Writing Room, Oxford University Poetry Society, Off the Chest, Gutter Street – and all the other poetry collectives and communities I have been blessed enough to be part of.

Thank you to the poets who have moved me, and whose forms, styles and words appear throughout this collection: Zeina Hashem Beck, Inua Ellams, Safia Elhillo, Terrance Hayes, Tishani Doshi, the list is endless.

Thank you to my illustrator, Peonica Fernando, for the stunning depiction of my grandmother, for taking my book and making it shine

And finally thank you to my publisher, Verve Poetry Press, and especially to Stuart for your belief, perseverance and passion, for making this project, this world, possible.

Earlier versions of some of these poems have appeared in *Bath Magg; The ISIS Magazine, Lacuna Lit; Modern Poetry in Translation; Poetry and Shaah* and *Wasafiri*.

ABOUT VERVE POETRY PRESS

Verve Poetry Press is a quite new and already award-winning press that focused initially on meeting a local need in Birmingham - a need for the vibrant poetry scene here in Brum to find a way to present itself to the poetry world via publication. Co-founded by Stuart Bartholomew and Amerah Saleh, it now publishes poets from all corners of the UK - poets that speak to the city's varied and energetic qualities and will contribute to its many poetic stories.

Added to this is a colourful pamphlet series, many featuring poets who have performed at our sister festival - and a poetry show series which captures the magic of longer poetry performance pieces by festival alumni such as Polarbear, Matt Abbott and Genevieve Carver.

The press has been voted Most Innovative Publisher at the Saboteur Awards, and has won the Publisher's Award for Poetry Pamphlets at the Michael Marks Awards.

Like the festival, we strive to think about poetry in inclusive ways and embrace the multiplicity of approaches towards this glorious art.

www.vervepoetrypress.com
@VervePoetryPres
mail@vervepoetrypress.com